ST. MARK SCHOOL

D0464076

Bo
Jackson
Playing the Games

Bo Jackson
Playing the Games

Ellen Emerson White

AN
APPLE
PAPERBACK

SCHOLASTIC INC.
New York Toronto London Auckland Sydney

Acknowledgments

I would like to thank everybody who helped me with this book. My particular thanks go to Jim Samia, Dick Bresciani, and the Boston Red Sox; John Wathan and the Kansas City Royals; Regina Griffin; and Sarah White.

Photo Credits

cover: Chuck Solomon/Sports Illustrated (above); Richard Mackson/ Sports Illustrated (below)

interior: Jerry Lodriguss/Sports Illustrated; © Kenneth Jarecke/Contact Press Images; © Kenneth Jarecke/Contact Press Images; John Iacono/ Sports Illustrated; © Kenneth Jarecke/Contact Press Images; © Kenneth Jarecke/Contact Press Images; © Kenneth Jarecke/Contact Press Images

No part of this publication may be reproduced in whole or in part, or stored in a retrieval system, or transmitted in any form or by any means, electronic, mechanical, photocopying, recording, or otherwise, without written permission of the publisher. For information regarding permission, write to Scholastic Inc., 730 Broadway, New York, NY 10003.

ISBN 0-590-44075-6

Copyright © 1990 by Ellen Emerson White.
All rights reserved. Published by Scholastic Inc.

12 11 10 9 8 7   3 4 5/9

Printed in the U.S.A.   40

First Scholastic printing, December 1990

*For my friend
Eve Hirst.
She knows books.*

Contents

Introduction

Everybody knows that Bo knows baseball. Bo knows football. Bo knows guitar playing. And, the truth is, Bo probably *does* know hockey. And bowling. And shuffleboard. And darts.

Many professional athletes are big and strong. Many professional athletes are fast. Very few of them are *both*. Bo Jackson can step up to the plate and hit a home run that would make Babe Ruth's jaw drop open. Then, in his next at bat, Bo is fully capable of bunting his way to first — and then stealing second, third, and home. He can catch fly balls other outfielders would never have reached, and then throw out the speediest runners trying to score from third base. In fact, it probably wouldn't surprise anyone to see Bo make a diving catch, scramble up, throw the ball home — and then run in, in time to catch his own throw and tag the runner out.

Bo's football skills are equally amazing. He can sprint past a fleet-footed defensive back like the 49ers' Ronnie Lott on one play, and then turn around and bulldoze right over a huge lineman like Buffalo's Bruce Smith on the next play.

What makes all of this even *more* amazing is that Bo goes from one professional sport straight to the other, with little more than a week's vacation in between. Other athletes have tried to succeed at more than one professional sport — most notably, the great Jim Thorpe — but not even Jim Thorpe was able to be a *star* in more than one professional sport. It is easy to imagine Bo hitting the game-winning home run in the World Series, and then scoring the winning touchdown in the Super Bowl three months later. In any given year, he could be the Most Valuable Player in baseball's All-Star Game *and* football's Pro Bowl. Bo makes the incredible seem routine.

There has never been another athlete quite like Bo Jackson. There probably never will be.

1
The Legend Begins

Vincent Edward (Bo) Jackson was born on November 30, 1962. He grew up in the small town of Bessemer, Alabama, near Birmingham. Bo is the eighth of ten children, all of whom were brought up by their mother, Florence Bond. Although Bo's father lived nearby, he rarely involved himself with his family. As a result, Florence had to work very hard to support her children.

With his mother working long hours as a chambermaid at a local Holiday Inn, Bo had plenty of time to make mischief. Making mischief was probably the first thing at which Bo excelled. In fact, it would be fair to say that he was something of a bully. He lost the name "Vincent" early in life, when his three big brothers started calling him "Boar Hog," which was short for "as mean as a boar hog," an old Southern expression. Over the years, his nickname evolved into just plain "Bo."

Today, very few people even know that Bo's real name is Vincent, and his wife, Linda, is one of the only people in the world who calls him by his real name. His mother named him Vincent because she liked the actor Vince Edwards, who starred in the television series *Ben Casey*.

While growing up, Bo was very energetic and hard to discipline. He had a reputation for being the troublemaker of his neighborhood and was often involved in fights and petty theft. One of Bo's brothers had spent some time in reform school, and he tried to keep his little brother from going the same way, but Bo continued to get into trouble. Sometimes Bo stuttered — especially when teachers would call on him in class — and he would always start a fight with anyone who made fun of him.

Although Bo played Little League baseball, sports were not yet very important to him. His mother often scolded him and tried to get him to mend his ways, but Bo's rambunctious behavior continued. Then, when he was almost fourteen, something happened that changed Bo's life.

It was summer, and Bo was fooling around with a group of his friends. They ended up at a nearby farm, where they vandalized a lot of property, causing a great deal of damage. Because of Bo's reputation for being a troublemaker, everyone knew who he was, and he was the only boy who was recognized when he and his friends ran away from the farm. All of the boys got away — except for Bo.

The owner of the farm was a minister, who, instead of pressing charges, suggested that Bo be grounded for the summer and spend his time doing chores, so he could pay the minister for the damages. Bo's family was very relieved, since he could have been sent to reform school. Aware that he had had a very close call, Bo decided it was time to shape up. This made his mother very happy, since she had spent a lot of time worrying about her son's future.

As Bo started high school, his future began to seem more clear. Bo discovered sports. With such a big family, Bo had always played games, but high school varsity sports were different. High school varsity sports were serious. And Bo was a natural.

From the very first, Bo was able to star at every athletic endeavor he attempted. Most professional athletes have to practice and practice for many years to learn their sport, but Bo always hated practicing, and he still does today. For Bo, it was competition, and actual games, that mattered. Practice bored him, and he rarely performed well until the umpire said, "Batter up!"

or the referee blew the whistle, or the starter's pistol went off. Bo only liked to play when it counted.

At the beginning, this attitude was hard for his coaches to understand; but once they saw Bo in action, they just let Bo do what he wanted to do. Blue moons come around more often than athletes like Bo Jackson.

Bo played three varsity sports in high school: football, baseball, and track. He was selected as an All-Stater in all three, a truly remarkable achievement. Track was probably his favorite of the three sports, and he was the top sprinter in the entire state of Alabama.

One thing Bo's coaches noticed about him was that he did everything necessary to win — and nothing more. Many sports observers feel that Bo still has this attitude today, which means that Bo may be capable of even more incredible achievements than he has already demonstrated. Bo may well be capable of things he will never show — unless, of course, the game is on the line.

Bo went to McAdory High School in McCalla, Alabama. His hometown of Bessemer was too small to have a high school of its own. Bo's mother didn't like the fact that he played football — she thought that it was much too dangerous and wanted to see him concentrate on baseball or track. In fact, she would threaten to lock him out of the house if he played football, especially if he came home hurt. She wasn't going to kick her son out permanently, but she wanted to make it clear that she didn't approve of such a rough game.

But Bo liked football. Bo liked football so much that he played halfback, tailback, fullback, defensive end, kicker *and* kick-returner. The only thing Bo *didn't* do was march in the band during halftime. Despite his versatility, it was clear that Bo was at his best as a running back, and he was considered one of the finest high school halfbacks in Alabama. He gained a total of 1,173 yards on 108 carries, for a terrific average gain of almost 11 yards in his senior year.

Bo also liked track — even more than he liked football. One thing Bo had always been was fast. In his freshman year, he entered the state decathlon meet. This is a track event where athletes compete in ten different events, including hurdles, the high jump, the long jump, the shot put, the discus, the pole vault, and the mile run. Bo had never thrown a shot put or a discus before, or even attempted to pole vault, but he went ahead and entered anyway — and came in tenth in the state. In his junior and senior years of high school, Bo was the Alabama high school state decathlon champion. This, despite the fact that he didn't bother competing in one of the events — the mile run — because he was already so far ahead of everyone else in points that he didn't *have* to take part in it — he could still win. Bo's coaches knew better than to argue with him.

Bo's statistics in the decathlon his final year in high school were just plain amazing — especially for a guy who rarely practiced. Bo was the sort of athlete who wouldn't bother jumping over real hurdles, if he could jump over folding chairs instead. His time in the 100-meter run was one-hundredth of a second too slow to qualify for the national Olympic trials. One-hundredth of a second is not very long. Bo threw the shot put over 50 feet and hurled the discus over 150 feet. His normal triple jump was just over 44 feet, but when another competitor jumped 47 feet and 8 inches, Bo jumped again, going 48 feet and a little more than 8 inches. Once again, Bo did just enough to win — who knows how far he could have jumped if he had really wanted to try. Bo is the ultimate example of "anything you can do, I can do better."

By the time Bo's high school track career was over, he had set state records in the 60- and 120-yard hurdles, the 60- and 100-yard dashes, the long jump, the high jump, and the decathlon.

Bo also, of course, liked baseball. He didn't really enjoy pitching — but, he still had a 9–1 record as a pitcher his final year. Judging from his performance that year, his motto must have been: "When in doubt, strike 'em out." But Bo liked to hit much better. In his senior year, his batting average was close to .450, and he hit twenty home runs, which set a national high school record. Bo managed to set this national record even though he missed *seven* games so that he could run in various track meets. Baseball scouts were disappointed more than once, as they arrived to watch a McAdory High School game, to find that Bo had decided he would rather run in a track meet on that particular day. Run, and *win*, more likely than not.

As graduation came closer, Bo had some decisions to make. For one thing, the New York Yankees had drafted him in the second round of that year's (1982) baseball free-agent draft. The Major League Scouting Bureau had listed Bo as one of the finest potential prospects to come along in years. The Yankees offered Bo a quarter of a million dollars to come and play in their minor league system. Bo was tempted by this, but his mother wanted him to go to college. So that's what Bo decided to do.

No one in Bo's family had ever attended a major university, and it was important to his mother that he take advantage of the chance to further his education. The question was, where? Many colleges and universities expressed interest, but Bo wanted to go to the University of Alabama and play for the legendary football coach Bear Bryant. Unfortunately — for Alabama — Bo found out that he was going to start his college career on the bench. Bo had no interest in *that*, so when Auburn University's football coach Pat

Dye assured him that he would be a starter, Bo knew where he wanted to go. He had also been promised that he would be able to play baseball and run on the track team, in addition to his football duties. So, Bo became an Auburn Tiger.

It was a very big step toward his future.

2
Big Man on Campus

Bo's reputation preceded him to Auburn University, and he was the center of attention from the moment he stepped on campus. Auburn was especially happy to get him since the University of Alabama was their archrival in the Southeastern Conference. Auburn and the University of Alabama have both always been college football powerhouses. Both universities are in the state of Alabama, and by this time, just about everyone in Alabama had heard of Bo Jackson. Still self-conscious about the speech impediment he'd grown up with, Bo found all of this campus scrutiny difficult.

Adjusting to college life — Bo had decided he would major in child and family development — was hard enough, but Bo soon found

11

something that was even harder: the Auburn Creed.

George Petrie, who had coached the Auburn football team back in 1892, had come up with this creed, which was taken very seriously by the athletic department. The creed said, "I believe that this is a practical world, and that I can count only on what I earn. Therefore, I believe in work, hard work."

Auburn football coach Pat Dye and his assistants also believed in hard work. Bo, the natural athlete who had never been one to practice or do calisthenics, did not feel the same way. His new coaches made him spend so much time practicing that Bo decided football wasn't much fun anymore, and halfway through his first semester he almost quit school. In fact, legend has it that Bo actually went to the bus station and sat there for several hours, deciding whether or not to go home to Bessemer. In the end, he decided to stay in school.

The Auburn coaches decided to change their attitudes as has every coach who has ever coached Bo, and to let Bo be Bo. They had never dealt with an athlete quite like him before, and it took both sides some time to adjust. In the end, Bo happily suited up in his blue-and-orange uniform, wearing the number 34. His coaches just sat back and marveled at an athlete who could bench press over 400 pounds — but never lifted weights; an athlete who was in perfect physical shape, but who constantly ate junk food; an athlete big enough to run through a brick wall, but fast enough to run through the rain without getting wet.

After the football season was over, Bo ran indoor track. His two main events were the 60-yard dash, and the 4 x 100-meter team relay. Later that season, he was a semifinalist in the NCAA championships in the 60-yard dash.

Once the track season was over, it was time for baseball. Bo had to miss spring training because he was still running on the track team and, as a result, he was a little rusty when the baseball season began. He was *so* rusty that he struck out the first 21 times he came to the plate. But, in 26 total games, he ended up with a .279 average. This was mediocre by Bo's standards, but quite respectable after such a terrible start. In baseball, he wore the number 29.

Regardless of his hitting woes, the major league scouts who attended his games were very impressed. Bo's speed, combined with his arm strength and batting power, made him a player with phenomenal potential. Bo is a right-handed batter who can run from home plate to first base in 3.8 seconds — which is a full half-second faster than most *left*-handed batters in the big leagues. (A left-handed batter is about a step-and-a-half closer to first, so he is able to get there that much faster.) Mickey Mantle and Willie Mays were the only two pro baseball players in history with the same combination of incredible speed and power. Bo was in pretty good company.

In Bo's sophomore year, he felt much more relaxed with his football coaches, and he had a terrific season. He rushed for over 1,200 yards, with a 7.7-yards-per-carry average. The football team won 11 games that year and lost only one, Bo leading his Tigers to the Southeastern Conference championship. He scored 12 touchdowns and was selected as an All-America.

Auburn went to the Sugar Bowl that year, where they beat Michigan by a score of 9–7. Michigan was noted for its defense, and they had been keeping entire *teams* below 100 yards rushing per game. In the Sugar Bowl, Bo rushed for 130 yards, and he was chosen the Most Valuable Player of the game.

Phil Snow, an Alabama sports reporter for station WSFA, covered Bo throughout his college career. "Bo was very serious about his football," Phil said, "but he was also serious about his academics. After games, even though he had a speech impediment, he was always willing to talk. He has since overcome that impediment, probably because he was constantly dealing with the media and having to talk. After almost every game, they would have to hold a press conference just for Bo."

Never one to take time off, Bo went straight from football to track. He didn't like Auburn's baseball coach, and so he decided to run both indoor and outdoor track that year, and skip baseball altogether. Once again, he went to the NCAA national championships, where he came in seventh.

Bo was invited to the Millrose Games that January, and he was very excited because they were to be held in New York City, a place where he had never been. Although he enjoyed seeing the city, he didn't do very well in the track meet, placing only sixth in the preliminary heat, and failing to qualify for the finals.

Later on, in the 1984 Florida Relays, Bo posted an almost world-class 10.13 seconds in the 100-meter run. This was a millisecond too slow to qualify for the Olympics. That season, in one meet, he ran his best time to date in the 60-yard dash, a blinding 6.18 seconds. (Carl Lewis holds the world indoor record in this event, with a time of 6.02 seconds.) So, once again, Bo was right up there with the best sprinters in the world.

Bo was also enjoying his studies, spending a lot of time at the Auburn Child Study Center, playing with children. Another reason he enjoyed hanging around the Center was because he had met a young woman named Linda, who is now his wife. At this writing, they have two children: Garrett (also called "Spud") and Nicholas, with a third on the way. Linda was also majoring in child study, and today she is working on her doctorate at Auburn, planning a career in counseling children. Bo has often been quoted as saying that

15

he expects to join his wife in this career when he retires from professional sports.

"Bo doesn't fit the stereotype of the athlete," reporter Phil Snow said. "I think he's well grounded as a person. He's a very moral person. He's more of a role model than most athletes today. He's very conservative in his behavior and very close to his family."

While at college, Bo spent much of his free time with Linda, and he used the rest of his free time to walk by himself in the woods. Sometimes he would hunt or fish; sometimes he would just roam around. Today, this is one of the main ways he gets away from the pressures of professional sports and worldwide celebrity.

It was now Bo's junior year, and the football team was hoping that he would lead them to another championship. The season didn't start off very well and got much worse in a game against the Texas Longhorns. Bo, who was limping from a sprained ankle he had suffered in a game against the University of Miami the week before, was determined to have a good game and help his team win.

In the third quarter, Bo broke away for a long run, strewing enemy defenders in his path. He had gone 53 yards and was on his way to a touchdown, when Texas safety Jerry Grey — a friend of Bo's and fellow All-America — tackled him. Bo got up, not realizing that he had suffered a very serious injury.

He stayed in the game for seven more plays, actually rushing the football three times, and receiving repeated hard tackles. Finally the pain was so bad that he had to leave the game. The team flew him back to Auburn, where he was examined by doctors, who discovered that he had completely separated his shoulder and would need immediate surgery. It was the first bad injury of Bo's entire sports career, and he didn't like being in the hospital. He also didn't like the fact that his team lost the game to Texas, 35–27.

The doctors said that Bo would have to miss at least eight weeks, and probably the rest of the football season. Bo's teammates rallied and won their next several games, and Bo returned only seven weeks after his operation.

In his first game back, against rival Alabama, Bo played as though he had never been hurt. He scored a touchdown and ran for 118 yards. It was as though he had never been gone. He played in at least a portion of each of the team's last three games, and Auburn was chosen to play in the Liberty Bowl.

Their opponent was the University of Arkansas. Bo rose to the occasion, rushing for 88 yards and scoring two touchdowns, to lead his team to a 21–15 win. He was selected, predictably, as the game's Most Valuable Player. Despite his injury,

Bo had had a good season, rushing for another 1,200 yards.

He decided to take it easy — by his standards — and not run track that winter. But Auburn had hired a new baseball coach, Hal Baird, and Bo liked him very much. So, this year, he went back to the baseball team. He had an excellent season, hitting .401, with 17 homeruns and 43 runs batted in (RBIs), in only 42 games. He still struck out a few too many times, but when he *did* make contact, he hit a sizzling .557.

There was one game that season that people are still talking about today. It was a game against the University of Georgia — the first night game in the Georgia Bulldogs' history. The way Bo played that night, it was almost the *last* night game in Georgia history.

There was a big crowd, by college standards, on hand that night, including many baseball scouts and reporters. Bo grounded out the first time he was up, but in his second at bat he hit a monumental home run — a home run too grand even for a Hollywood movie. He sent the ball far into the night, to the deepest part of center field, and when it went out of the park, it was still about a hundred feet off the ground, apparently heading for outer space. But the light tower got in the way. The ball hit the tower with a great crash and shattering of glass, and people could not quite believe their eyes. If it weren't for the light tower — what was left of it — the ball would probably still be traveling.

The next time Bo came up, he hit another home run — a normal home run, but still mighty impressive. When he came up again, the crowd held its breath, and Bo hit a *third* home run. In his final at bat he only hit a double — *only* — and the crowd actually booed in disappointment.

With achievements like these, the world of professional sports came even closer, and that summer, Bo had two tough choices to make. He had watched friends like Herschel Walker and Marcus Dupree leave college early to sign football contracts in the (no longer existing) United States Football League. Bo got a serious offer from the USFL's Birmingham Stallions, and he strongly considered taking it.

Then, the California Angels selected him in the first round of the major league baseball draft that year — the second time he had been drafted by a big league club. The Angels had made him the twenty-second pick overall, and Bo's favorite player Reggie Jackson would be his teammate. Bo was very tempted.

However, his mother wanted him to finish college. So, despite the huge salaries the pros were offering, Bo decided to go back to school for his final year.

It was a good decision.

3
Going for the Heisman

Bo wanted his final college football season to be his very best, and it certainly was. Pat Dye and his assistant coaches had developed a special I-formation to help showcase their star running back's abilities. An I-formation is when the football offense sets up so that the running backs are directly behind the quarterback. This way, the running backs are far enough back to be able to read the other team's defensive setup and plan their moves — and close enough to the quarterback to be able to get the ball quickly. There are many other ways for an offense to set up — such as the shotgun formation, to take advantage of a great quarterback's arm; the wishbone formation, for a more balanced running and passing attack; and the open set, where the players are spread out across the field, so that any one of the number of different plays can take place. But a team with a great running back will usually focus on the I-formation, which looks exactly the way it sounds; as does the wishbone.

So, everything was in place for Bo to have a terrific season. In three of his first four games, he rushed for over 200 yards, and Bo was clearly in the running for the 1985 Heisman Trophy, an award given to the best college player in the country, as voted by over a thousand sportswriters. Winning the Heisman is a very big honor.

Bo had some tough competition. Chuck Long, the quarterback for the University of Iowa, was having a great year, as were Lorenzo White, a Michigan State running back, and Vinny Testaverde, the University of Miami quarterback. But Bo had a better year.

He did miss a couple of games — both of which Auburn lost — because of a pulled thigh muscle. Many people in the sports world grumbled that Bo wasn't much of a team player if he wouldn't play hurt. But they didn't know that Bo had cracked some ribs in Auburn's final game of the year against Alabama, and played anyway, gaining 149 yards. Old-fashioned sports observers complain when players won't "play hurt," but it takes a mature and intelligent athlete to realize that it is better to miss a game or two than to aggravate an injury. When an injured athlete tries to play through the injury, he or she often makes it worse. A smart athlete knows better — and Bo is a smart athlete.

Auburn didn't win the SEC championship that year, but they were good enough to go to the Cotton Bowl. Bo's statistics for the season were almost superhuman. He gained 1,786 yards for a 6.4 yards-per-gain average. He scored 17 touchdowns, and in one game, against Southwestern Louisiana, he rushed for an unbelievable 290 yards. He ran for over 100 yards in eight games, setting an Auburn record. He averaged 162.4 yards per game, and a mind-boggling 9.3 points per game.

Unfortunately Bo and his teammates didn't do very well in the Cotton Bowl. They were playing against Texas A & M, a team famous for its so-called "twelfth man," meaning its wildly partisan and noisy crowd. The crowd had often been credited for influencing the outcome of Texas A & M games, and the Cotton Bowl was no exception.

Bo ran for 129 yards that day, and caught two passes for 73 yards. He scored two touchdowns in the first half and helped set up an Auburn field goal in the third quarter.

In the fourth quarter, Auburn was on the two-yard line, and only five points down, with a good chance to win. The quarterback gave Bo the ball three times in a row, but he couldn't score. In the crucial fourth quarter, he was stopped for no gain on five consecutive plays. Auburn lost the game, and Bo and his teammates were very disappointed. But that didn't change the fact that Bo had had a very special season.

Bo's final college statistics were outstanding. He was the first running back in Auburn history to rush for more than 4,000 yards, ending up with 4,303; averaging 6.6 yards per carry over his college career. In 38 total games, he averaged 113.2 yards per game, and scored 45 touchdowns. In the 40-yard run — a common football skills test — Bo had finished in 4.13 seconds. To put that number in perspective, 4.4 seconds is considered *excellent* in the National Football League. Bo was that much faster. With all that speed, and all that bulk, he was certain to be one of the first choices in the NFL draft.

But first, Bo won a couple of awards. He was selected to the All-America team again, but he also received the Walter Camp Trophy for the most outstanding college football player in the country. Walter Camp, who played for Yale in the 1800s, had created the first All-America team back in 1879, and the annual award was a tribute to his memory.

The vote for the 1985 Heisman Trophy was surprisingly close, considering the numbers Bo had produced during his season. Many people feel that Bo lost a few votes because of those two games missed as a result of his pulled muscle. Over one thousand ballots were cast, and the vote was the closest in the 51 years of the Heisman

Trophy's existence. Bo won, with 1,509 points, beating Chuck Long, the Iowa quarterback, who received 1,464 points, after having led his team to the Rose Bowl. Robbie Bosco, the Brigham Young University quarterback, came in third that year, with running back Lorenzo White and quarterback Vinny Testaverde rounding out the pack. Bo was the winner of the most prestigious prize in college football, an honor he proudly accepted at the Downtown Athletic Club in New York City.

Then, not one to rest on his laurels, Bo started getting ready for the baseball season. Midway through his season, something happened that may have changed the course of athletic history. It was expected that the Tampa Bay Buccaneers would use the first pick in the NFL draft to select Bo. Failing that, the Atlanta Falcons would *definitely* choose him, with their second pick of the draft. Tampa Bay owner Hugh Culverhouse sent his jet to Auburn to fly Bo down to Florida for a pre-draft physical, a precaution professional teams like to take.

Naturally Bo passed with flying colors, but when he returned to Auburn, he discovered that he had lost his amateur eligibility, according to a somewhat obscure rule used in the Southeastern Conference. In most college conferences (but not the SEC), a player is allowed to play one sport professionally, and another sport on an amateur basis. The SEC decided that Bo's accepting a free plane ride to Florida made him a professional, even though he hadn't signed anything — or even been drafted yet. Therefore, barely halfway into the season, Bo had to drop off the Auburn baseball team. He had had only 69 at bats, striking out 29 times, hitting seven home runs, and finishing with a rather low .246 average. He was disappointed by these numbers, but he was even *more* disappointed that he wasn't allowed to play baseball anymore.

Bo had been unaware that there would be a problem if he visited Tampa Bay, and this was a detail that the Tampa Bay ownership should have checked. If they had, Bo would probably be wearing a Tampa Bay uniform today, and not playing professional baseball at all. But someone was a little bit sloppy, and this was something that Bo — who just wanted to finish out his baseball season — wasn't likely to forget.

It was almost time for the NFL draft, and Tampa Bay had managed to upset the best college player in the country. It was a mistake that they aren't likely to forget, either.

4
Decision Time

As expected, Tampa Bay made Bo the first pick in the NFL draft. What happened next was *un*-expected. Everyone in the sporting world assumed that Bo Jackson, the Heisman Trophy winner, would certainly play football. It would be a complete waste of time for a baseball team to spend a draft pick on him. However, the Kansas City Royals did, making Bo their pick in the fourth round of the baseball draft, and the one-hundred-and-fourth pick overall.

On June 21, 1986, Bo and his agent, Richard Woods, held a press conference in Birmingham to announce that Bo would be signing a contract to play with the Royals. The media were stunned.

For one thing, word had leaked out that the Tampa Bay Buccaneers were going to offer Bo at least 7.6 million dollars, spread out over five years. Bo would be the first-string running back from the moment he stepped onto the field, and he would be certain to be a star in his first season.

What did baseball have to offer? Rumor had it that the Royals were going to give Bo only $100,000, plus $100,000 more as a signing bonus. He would go straight to the minors, and possibly spend as long as three or four years working his way up to the big leagues. He would travel on long, bumpy bus rides, eat fast food, and play on poorly maintained fields in front of tiny crowds. The minor leagues were not very glamorous, and not very lucrative.

The last Heisman Trophy winner not to sign a professional football contract had been Pete Dawkins, back in 1958, who had gone into the military instead. What sane athlete would give up the glory and financial rewards of a football career for the lonely drudgery of working his way up through baseball's minor leagues? And what baseball team would be foolish enough to sign Bo, when he would probably change his mind and go play football anyway?

Kansas City was the only team stupid enough — or *wise* enough — to take the chance. Credit must be given to Ewing Kauffman, the co-owner of the Royals, and John Schuerholz, the Royals' general manager, for taking the risk. And the risk paid off.

Why *did* Bo decide to go with baseball when

he could make so much more money playing football? Well, if money had been important to him, he would have signed with the Yankees after high school, or gone to the Angels when they drafted him after his junior year in college. Certainly, baseball is a more relaxed, lighthearted game than football is. Baseball is almost — gentle. The chances of serious injury are much lower in pro baseball than they are in the NFL.

Also, Bo was still upset with Tampa Bay for causing him to lose his college baseball eligibility. Another problem with Tampa Bay was that they weren't a very good team. Bo wanted to play for a team — in baseball or football — that was good enough to have a chance for the Super Bowl or the World Series, and a team that was in a city where the weather was nice and warm. Tampa Bay only qualified in one of those categories.

So, Bo signed a three-year contract with the Royals, insisting that clauses be put into the contract stipulating that he would repay *all* of the money Kansas City had given him if he, for some reason, decided to leave baseball for football by July 15 of the following year. If he left baseball for football after July 15, 1987, he would return half of all the money he had been paid. The Kansas City management found this unselfish idea rather unexpected — but, delightful.

After Bo's press conference that June morning, he flew up to Kansas City to work out with the big league ball club. The Royals wanted to give their new prospect a taste of the big time. The plan was for Bo to work out with the big league club for a couple of weeks, and then be assigned to a club in the minor league system.

When Bo got off the plane, he didn't have any equipment, and he had to borrow everything from a bat and glove, to some shoes. He was given a uniform with number 16 on the jersey.

During his first batting practice, using a bat that belonged to designated hitter Steve Balboni, Bo hit a shot to the base of the Royals' scoreboard, at least 450 feet away, above the wall in deep center field. It is easy to imagine the smiles that must have been on the faces of the Kansas City coaches. The smiles must have gotten even wider when Bo hit five more home runs.

The Kansas City trainers gave Bo various strength and physical fitness tests, and Bo tested higher than any other athlete they had ever examined. In fact, at one point, one of the trainers testing Bo's arm strength found the numbers so high that he thought he had tested Bo's leg strength by mistake. Bo was like no athlete anyone had ever seen. He had the speed of a Ron Leflore or a Willie Wilson, the power of a Mickey Mantle or a Babe Ruth, and the arm of a Roberto Clemente or a Dwight Evans.

When it came time to be assigned to the minor leagues, Bo hoped he would be sent to the Triple-A club (the highest rung in the minors) in Omaha, but instead, the Royals sent him to their Double-

A club in the Southern League, the Memphis Chicks. The main things the Royals wanted him to work on were hitting the inside fastball, cutting down on his strikeouts, and improving his outfielding.

During batting practice on his first day with the Chicks, Bo hit four home runs on his first twelve swings. And there were more Kansas City coaches with big grins across their faces.

Bo made his professional baseball debut on June 30, in a game at Tim McCarver Stadium in Memphis, against the Columbus Astros. The park was jammed with reporters and spectators, including people from all the major networks and sports channels. It would have to be one of the most publicized minor league games in the history of baseball. Every eye in the park was on a young six-foot-one-inch, 220-pound man wearing number 28.

Bo's new manager, Tommy Jones, decided to place him seventh in the batting order, as the team's designated hitter. When Bo stepped up to the plate for his first professional at bat, the crowd — even the reporters — erupted into a standing ovation. Bo responded with an RBI single. Clearly Bo *knew* baseball.

Unfortunately Bo's next ten days or so with the Chicks weren't quite as successful. He only got one more hit — a pop fly double — in his next 26 at bats. It was beginning to look like the man whom the Major League Scouting Bureau had given a 75.5 rating — on a scale that considers a score of 70 or above to be a probable superstar — was going to have trouble hitting professional pitching.

Bo's adjustment to the minor leagues was difficult, particularly since he hadn't been able to play competitive baseball since early March when he lost his eligibility at Auburn. He was striking out, misplaying balls in the outfield — and he even got picked off first base. After 27 professional at bats, Bo found himself with an .047 batting average.

Then, on July 13, in a game against Charlotte, Bo hit his first professional home run, a three-run shot. After that things began to improve, and Bo made steady progress. The very next week, he was named Southern League Player-of-the-Week, after going 11 for 26, including two home runs, three triples, and eight runs batted in. In the last 40 games of the Chicks' season, Bo hit .338, including an eight-game hitting streak. It had been a rocky beginning, but now things were going Bo's way.

On September 1, the Royals called him up to the majors, making Bo the first player in Royals history to go from the college campus to the big leagues in the same year. On September 2, the Royals' manager stuck Bo right into the lineup.

The Royals were playing the Chicago White

Sox, and Steve Carlton — a sure Hall-of-Famer, with more than 300 career victories — was pitching.

When Bo came to the plate for the first time — the future star against the veteran star — he hit a grounder to the infield. The major leagues got their first look at Bo's astonishing speed as he beat it out for a hit. It was the only hit he got in the game, but it was a good start.

In Bo's fifth game, against the Seattle Mariners, Bo had *four* hits, becoming only the sixth rookie in Royals history to accomplish that feat. What made this even more impressive was that it only took him five games to do it.

Then, on September 14, while playing the Mariners at Royals Stadium, Bo hit his first home run off then Seattle pitcher Mike Moore. But this wasn't just any home run — it was the longest home run ever hit by a right-handed batter in Royals Stadium, landing over 475 feet away, beyond the left-center-field fence.

Two days later, Bo hit another home run, to tie the score in the eighth inning of a game against the California Angels. California went on to win the game, but the rookie had made it obvious that he was here to stay.

After only 89 college games, and 53 games in the minors, Bo Jackson was a big league baseball player. Soon, he would be a star.

5
A New Hobby

Bo went to spring training the next year, determined to stick with the major league roster. He played hard, and well, and on Opening Day, he was in the lineup as the Royals' left fielder.

During the first few weeks of the season, Bo was nothing less than awesome. He was batting .500 after his first 28 trips to the plate. The season had barely begun, and he had already smacked three home runs, and knocked in 13 runs. Bo was everything that had been advertised, and more.

On April 10, against the powerful New York Yankees, Bo had four hits. Then, a few days later against the Detroit Tigers, he had another four-hit game. Two of these four hits were home runs, including a grand slam. Bo tied a long-standing

Kansas City record by driving in seven runs in that game.

In fact, the only sour note during the entire month of April was the night that Bo struck out five times in a single game. As is true for any free-swinging power hitter, Bo still had a tendency to strike out a lot.

On April 28, Bo's batting average was a terrific .344, with four home runs and fifteen RBIs. However, a funny thing happened on that day. The 1987 National Football League draft took place, and the Los Angeles Raiders — in a seemingly wacky move — drafted Bo in the seventh round. Observers agreed that this was a complete waste of a pick by Los Angeles, and that Tampa Bay had been wise not to redraft Bo and retain their rights to him. After all, he was a major league baseball player now.

Indeed, Bo continued to have a pretty successful rookie season. He still needed to work on being more selective at the plate, and avoiding the tendency to swing wildly, but all in all, the Royals' management was very pleased with their young star.

The media, of course, speculated about why the Los Angeles Raiders had thrown away a draft pick, and whether Bo might be considering a change. Bo and his agent — and the Royals — and the Raiders — weren't talking.

Bo continued to put up impressive statistics.

He hit two home runs against Texas in a game in May; he had another two-homer game against Seattle in early June.

By mid-July, Bo was hitting .253, with 18 home runs and 45 RBIs. He also had 112 strikeouts. If he continued at that pace, he would break the all-time major league strikeout record, set by Bobby Bonds, who had 189 strikeouts back in 1970. (Since the 1987 season, Pete Incaviglia, of the Texas Rangers, has broken that strikeout record.) This was very frustrating for Bo.

One Friday night in Toronto, after striking out a couple of times, Bo was taken out of the game — although the Royals lost, anyway. Naturally, he found this quite upsetting.

Ironically — considering his lack of success the night before — Bo held a press conference the next day. A roomful of eager reporters gathered to hear what he was going to say. An amazed silence fell — followed by a battery of questions — when Bo told the press that he had signed a five-year contract worth more than two-and-a-half-million dollars to play for the Los Angeles Raiders. The reporters were even more amazed when Bo explained that he would continue to play baseball, and would not join the Raiders until after his season with the Royals was completed each year.

Then Bo made an unfortunate remark, which would come back to haunt him for quite some time. While trying to make it clear that he was a Kansas City Royal first, and a football player second, Bo said that football would merely be a hobby for him, like hunting or fishing.

This did not go over very well.

The media thought that that was a very arrogant thing to say, and blasted Bo in their stories, writing sarcastically about some other hobbies he might try — like stamp collecting. Many NFL football players were angry and offended that Bo had apparently belittled their sport, and they made a lot of comments about the fact that Bo would have a few surprises coming when he put on his Los Angeles Raider uniform. Many baseball players were upset — especially Bo's teammates. Baseball contracts are almost always very specific about what baseball players can and cannot do in the off-season. There are many restrictions, usually put in to protect the baseball team's investment, and to try to keep players from getting injured. And here Bo was, planning to play *football*, of all things, when most players were forbidden to ski or ride motorcycles or do any one of a number of dangerous activities. Playing football, most of Bo's teammates felt, was just looking for trouble.

Bo was surprised by the intensity of the reaction to his announcement. After all, the Royals' management had agreed to let him play football, and the Raiders had agreed that he could skip training camp and the first few games of every football season in order to fulfill his baseball commitments. The owners of each team were sensible enough to realize that Bo was no ordinary athlete, and that the ordinary rules just weren't going to work. Team officials, in both cases, knew that if they tried to prevent Bo from playing the other sport, he was fully capable of quitting. The one thing Bo had always made clear was that he didn't like to be pushed around, or told what to do. Both teams agreed that having even part of Bo Jackson was a lot better than having no Bo Jackson.

Although Bo was surprised by his teammates' reaction, the reaction of the Kansas City fans was even more upsetting. The Raiders were the deadly rivals of the Kansas City Chiefs, and the fans thought that Bo was the worst kind of traitor to sign on with the enemy.

When the Royals came home to play their first game after a long road trip, the fans booed Bo's every appearance. Many fans brought small plastic footballs to the stadium, which they threw onto the field — and at Bo. They chanted, "It's a hobby, it's a hobby!" and booed wildly. Bo did his best to accept all of this with a sense of humor, but it was very difficult.

Kansas City lost that first game to the Orioles, and Bo went 0 for 3, with two strikeouts. In fact, Bo really didn't play very well for the rest of the season. People blamed this on the fact that he was concentrating on the upcoming football season, rather than on his baseball, but the relentless resentment Bo was getting from every direction probably had a lot more to do with his slump.

Bo finished the season with a team-high 158 strikeouts, spending 37 of the team's last 54 games on the bench. He ended up with a .235 batting average, 22 home runs, and 53 RBIs. He had averaged one strikeout for every 2.51 at bats. But, interestingly enough, it turned out that when Bo *did* connect with the ball, his average was .391. This was comparable to Wade Boggs of the Boston Red Sox, whose contact average was .398. Considering that Boggs, year after year, won the American League batting title, Bo was in pretty good company. In fact, with a .391 contact average, he placed seventh among all major leaguers that year. Despite his rather low batting average, this was a comforting statistic.

"He can get better than he has shown," Kansas City hitting coach Mike Lum said. "I think he will hit for average, if he can cut down on the strikeouts. It's obvious that if you can put more balls in play, you have a better chance of getting base hits."

Bo's rookie baseball season had had its ups and downs, but the fact that his 22 home runs were a record for a Royals' rookie was certainly an encouraging one. Ideally, the Royals would have liked to have him play winter ball in the Instructional League, and continue to work on fundamentals, but they knew that this was not a very realistic plan. After all, Bo was going to be very busy. Bo was going to be playing professional football.

6
Bo Knows Football

Very few athletes have ever tried to play more than one professional sport, and no one has ever been terribly successful at the attempt. Not only does a player need incredible physical ability to do such a thing, but he or she also needs tremendous mental toughness. The pressures and stresses of playing *one* professional sport are intense enough; it would seem almost impossible to play *two* professional sports.

The most famous athlete — before Bo — to play two pro sports was Jim Thorpe. A star football player, Jim also spent six seasons playing major league baseball. Jim had a legendary football career, but never hit higher than the mid-two-hundreds in baseball. As a baseball player, he was rather mediocre — comparatively speaking, of course. The most recent player to attemp to play both football and baseball was the 1954 Heisman Trophy winner, Vic Janowicz. Although he was a fine player for the Washington Redskins, his baseball career was not very impressive. Vic caught and played third base for the Pittsburgh Pirates, hitting .151 in 41 games, with only two RBIs.

Gene Conley played professional basketball and baseball during the fifties and early sixties, but he was never close to being a star in either sport. Dave DeBusschere was a spectacular basketball player for the New York Knicks during the sixties and early seventies, but his days as a pro baseball pitcher were not very memorable.

More recently, Danny Ainge played third base for the Toronto Blue Jays, but could never quite master the art of hitting the curveball. He went on to star for the Boston Celtics, and is currently playing for the Sacramento Kings.

It is worth noting that many of these athletes did not play two pro sports in the same year. Most of them went from one to the other, rather than trying to do both at the same time.

Currently, Deion Sanders is trying to play baseball with the New York Yankees, while playing football for the Atlanta Falcons. At this stage in his career, most observers would agree that Deion would be more successful in football.

Los Angeles Dodger Kirk Gibson was an All-America wide receiver at the University of Mich-

was drafted by the NFL's then-St. Louis
als, but he elected to play baseball instead.
er Broncos quarterback John Elway played
summer in the New York Yankees' farm sys-
m, but he probably never seriously considered
a baseball career in addition to his football career. Cincinnati Reds outfielder Eric Davis was a
very talented college basketball player, and could
probably have made it in the NBA.

All of the athletes mentioned above are very
gifted, but only Bo has Hall-of-Fame potential in
two sports. There aren't any athletes in the history of professional sports to whom Bo can be
compared.

After the baseball season ended on October 4,
Bo took a couple of weeks off, and then reported
to the Raiders. One nice thing about being drafted
by the Raiders was that one of Bo's former teammates from Auburn University, Chris Woods, also
played for Los Angeles. It would be nice for Bo
to go to a team where he already had an old
friend.

The Los Angeles Raiders (formerly the Oakland
Raiders) have long had a reputation for being a
rough and tough team — even by NFL standards.
They are no longer as good, or as rowdy, as they
were in years past, but the addition of a player
like Bo Jackson wasn't going to hurt them any.
In recent years, the Raiders' biggest problem has
been at quarterback, a position at which they
have made constant changes. A football team

42

needs stability at quarterback more than an other position, since, without question, the quarterback runs the show.

The Raiders wear black-and-silver uniforms. These colors help to remind people that they are a lean, mean fighting machine. Bo was assigned number 34.

The media were waiting eagerly for Bo to make his football debut, but Coach Tom Flores wanted him to take a couple of weeks to learn the offensive system and to get used to playing football again. After all, it had been quite a while since Bo had stepped onto a football field.

The Raiders were, so far, having a very poor 1987 season, losing far more often than they were winning. Coach Flores decided that Bo was ready to play in the November 1 game against the Patriots in Foxboro, Massachusetts.

The very first time Bo was given the ball, he rushed for 14 yards — a dramatic way to let everyone know that he was here in the NFL now, and that they had better pay attention to him. Even the Patriots' fans were impressed, and Bo got more than a few cheers.

Bo only carried the ball eight times — Coach Flores wanted to let him adjust to his new job gradually — for a total of 37 yards on the day. Bo also caught a pass for 6 yards.

It was a very exciting game. Nineteen eighty-seven was the year that the football players had been on strike to open the season, and once the s over, many teams had trouble getting to the swing of things. The Raiders and atriots were no exception to this. But on one fall day, both teams played hard, and both ams could have won.

Late in the game, the Patriots had a big lead, with their quarterback, Steve Grogan, passing for almost 300 yards. But late in the fourth quarter, the Raiders came back, and managed to tie the score at 23 apiece, with only 46 seconds to go.

The Patriots marched back down the field, to get within field goal range. Their kicker, Tony Franklin, missed an attempt from 34 yards, but then the Raiders were called for being offside. (Being offside is when someone on one of the teams moves too early. The team is automatically given a five-yard penalty, and the other team gets to take the play over, if they so choose.) The Patriots decided, naturally, to take the play over. This time, Franklin's kick was from 29 yards out, and he made it, giving the Patriots a 26–23 victory.

This was a bad way to lose a football game, and Bo and his teammates were very disappointed. The team's owner, Al Davis, was even more disappointed and vowed that changes were going to come at the quarterback position, if the team didn't start winning — and soon.

However, no one was disappointed with Bo's first day, as he had averaged a good 4.6 yards per carry. This was a very impressive start for a rookie.

The Raiders' next game was against the Minnesota Vikings. Bo had a pretty good day, but the Los Angeles quarterback, Steve Hilger, didn't, throwing three interceptions. Raiders owner Al Davis was so upset that he actually called down from the press box *during* the game and demanded that Coach Flores put in a new quarterback. Coach Flores sent Marc Wilson out to play, but it was too little, too late, and the Raiders lost the game, 31–20.

Bo ran for 74 yards that day, on 11 carries, and he also caught another pass for 7 yards. On one Raider drive, Bo did all the work, rushing for 9 yards, for 13 yards, and then for 20 yards. After that, Raider kicker Chris Bahr kicked a field goal. The only thing Bo did wrong was when he fumbled after catching the seven-yard pass. The Vikings recovered and ended up scoring a touchdown.

This game also pointed out a potential problem in the backfield. Before Bo joined the team, the Raiders already had a fantastic running back in veteran Marcus Allen. While no team can have too much talent, it is very hard to keep two premier running backs happy — each one can only carry the ball so many times, and a great running back really needs 20 or 30 carries a game. On this day, Bo had 12 carries, and Marcus had 11. A running back needs lots of chances so that he can get his rhythm and timing down in each particular game. It was going to be difficult to give both players enough work to stay sharp.

The Dallas Cowboys had recently faced the same problem — with unhappy results. Tony Dorsett had been their star running back for a number of years, and the offense essentially revolved around him. Then when the USFL folded, the Cowboys were able to sign Herschel Walker. The two players were unable to work together peacefully and, in the end, Dorsett went over to the Denver Broncos.

The Raiders wanted to avoid this situation at all costs. Luckily Marcus Allen made it clear that he was a team player first, and a running back second. If the team wanted him to play fullback, and spend most of his time blocking and setting up plays for Bo, then that was what he would do. This was a very admirable reaction, but it couldn't have been easy on Allen's ego.

In two games, Bo had rushed for 111 yards, with a sparkling 6.2-yards-per-carry average. He was on his way.

7
This Was No Rookie

Bo continued to play well over the next couple of games, but the Raiders continued to lose. The San Diego Chargers defeated them by a score of 16–14, as the Raiders' quarterbacking woes continued. Bo rushed for another 45 yards, while teammate Marcus Allen contributed 82. Bo was equally willing to serve as a blocking back if it would help the team, and the combination of his speed and strength was a powerful one.

Next, the Raiders played the Denver Broncos, and although they lost again, Bo had his best game to date. He rushed for 98 yards, and scored two touchdowns — the first of his professional career. He also, just to keep things interesting, caught five passes that day. Fellow running back Allen spent the entire day at fullback, but was able to gain 44 yards of his own.

After barely a month in the NFL, Bo was learning a few tricks. In his first couple of games, he had focused on using his speed to blow past enemy defenders. In this game, he decided to take advantage of weighing 225 pounds, and he started running *over* people, instead of around them. Bronco cornerback Mike Harden — who has gone to the Pro Bowl on more than one occasion — found this out as Bo ran right through him to score his first touchdown. This touchdown run was a remarkable one as Bo started to sweep around the right end, and then changed his mind and went left, sprinting for 35 yards before diving through Harden and into the end zone.

Quarterback Marc Wilson played well, completing 15 out of 21 passes, but Bronco quarterback John Elway was even better, passing for almost 300 yards. The Broncos won the game, 23–17.

The next time out, the Raiders finally broke their losing streak — and Bo had a game that would be spectacular by *any* standards. And because it was the Monday Night Football Game of the Week, a very big audience tuned in to witness his performance.

The game took place in Seattle's Kingdome, making Bo the first athlete in history to play both football *and* baseball in the Kingdome. (The Kingdome is the home field for both the Seattle Seahawks and the Seattle Mariners.)

It was November 30, which just happened to be Bo's twenty-fifth birthday. He celebrated the day in his own style. He scored three touchdowns to lead his team to victory, and each was amazing in its own way.

The first touchdown was a 91-yard run from the line of scrimmage, breaking the Raiders' all-time yardage record, set by Kenny King seven years earlier. Players often make long kickoff or punt returns, but a 90-plus-yard running play is a rarity. The great Jim Brown, the Hall of Fame running back to whom Bo is often compared, only had one such run in his entire nine-year career. Bo now had one after only five games in the NFL.

That touchdown was pretty impressive, but Bo's other rushing score was almost more so. It was a two-yard run, straight ahead, into the end zone. This does not sound very impressive, but to gain those two yards, Bo ran over Seattle's massive linebacker, Brian Bosworth. Bosworth — a huge man — was simply flattened.

Bo's third touchdown came on a 14-yard pass reception, which turned out to be his only catch of the day. But it was a pretty good one, as catches go, resulting in a score.

In 18 rushing attempts, Bo gained a total of 221 yards that night, breaking a 24-year-old Raiders' team record. He had a chance to break Walter Payton's all-time NFL single game rushing record of 275 yards, but Coach Flores decided to let Bo rest for the last half of the fourth quarter.

All in all, Bo had a very nice birthday, and the Raiders won by a final score of 37–14. If there was still anyone around who doubted that Bo knew football as well as he knew baseball, those doubts had now been permanently erased.

The Raiders continued their newfound winning ways in their next game, which was against the Buffalo Bills. The Bills' defense was so worried about containing Bo, that Raider quarterback Marc Wilson was able to pass almost at will, completing 21 passes for almost 340 yards, and three touchdowns. The Raiders won easily, 34–21.

Bo caught three passes for 36 yards and, just to break up the monotony, gained another 78 on the ground. To other people, football may have seemed like hard work, but Bo was just plain having fun.

The Raiders' next game was against their arch-rival, the Kansas City Chiefs. It would be played in Kansas City, in Arrowhead Stadium. Arrowhead Stadium and Royals Stadium are part of the same sports complex in Kansas City, thereby making Bo the first athlete ever to play in both stadiums. Bo was becoming, all by himself, the answer to a whole new group of sports trivia questions.

The game sold out early, and the press reported story after story about the irony and excitement of Bo coming to Kansas City as a member of the opposition. Another interesting aspect of the game was that the Chiefs had their own rookie star running back, Christian Okoye, a Nigerian player who had been setting a few records of his own. It would be a good match-up.

With so much anticipation building, the game could only be an anticlimax — and it was. The fans booed when Bo took the field and threw baseballs out of the stands. There were more than 200 banners displayed around the stadium referring to Bo and his supposed treachery in playing for the enemy.

On his very first run of the day, Bo sprained his ankle badly. He stayed in for a few more plays, but then had to leave the game. His total yardage for the day amounted to less than one yard. It was a disappointing end to Bo's day — and, as it turned out, to his season. His ankle was injured badly enough for him to miss the final two games of the year.

Without Bo, the Raiders started losing again. After the Chiefs beat them by a 16–10 score, they lost to the Cleveland Browns, and then to the Chicago Bears.

Bo was a unanimous choice for the NFL All-Rookie team, gaining a total of 554 yards for a 6.8-yards-per-carry average in his brief season. He had also caught 12 passes for a total of 85 yards. If he had played for the entire season, his numbers would probably have been even more remarkable — and, to this day, this is a constant sportswriters' complaint. Most reporters feel that

Bo would become the greatest running back in history — if he gave football his complete concentration. Then again, most people feel that Bo would be a cinch for baseball's Hall of Fame, too — if he gave baseball his entire attention. Despite Bo's fine performances in both sports, people still doubt him.

The numbers show that, clearly, Bo knew exactly what he was doing.

8
Next Stop, Kansas City

After his 1987 seasons, Bo became only the fifth athlete in history to hit a major league baseball home run and score a professional football touchdown in the same year. In fact, Bo had hit 22 home runs and scored six touchdowns.

In 1927, Pid Purdy hit a home run for the then Cincinnati Redlegs and scored a touchdown for the Green Bay Packers. Three years later, Red Badgro had scored two touchdowns for the New York Giants and hit a home run for the then St. Louis Browns baseball club. Ace Parker scored two touchdowns for Brooklyn's professional football team in 1937 and hit a home run for the Philadelphia Athletics. (The Philadelphia Athletics later became the Oakland A's.) Then, in 1945,

Steve Filipoqicz scored two touchdowns for football's New York Giants and hit two homers for baseball's New York Giants.

These were impressive feats to be sure, but none of these men ever became household names. Bo, in one season, had managed to hit many more home runs and score almost as many touchdowns as all four men put together. On top of which, Bo played less than half of a full football season. As far as the record books are concerned, Bo is in a category by himself.

Bo had less than two months before spring training and, amazingly, he was offered another job — just in case he wanted to use up some of that free time. Bo was offered a professional basketball contract. A new professional basketball league, called the International Basketball Association, was being established for players six feet four inches and under. The Orange Country Crush drafted Bo for their team, assuring him that he could play exclusively during the months of January and February. They even offered to send Harlem Globetrotter Meadowlark Lemon down to Bo's home in Alabama to coach him privately.

Bo declined this offer, saying that he would rather go fishing and hunting. Those two hobbies, plus football, were enough. Still, it would have been interesting to see if Bo could have become a professional basketball star as well.

Bo was a little nervous about spring training

that year. While he had been playing football, a young outfielder named Gary Thurman had been playing winter baseball — and playing very well. Ideally, the Royals had wanted Bo to play winter ball, too, and now Thurman had the inside track on left field. The Royals had been a little disappointed by Bo's slump during the second half of the 1987 season, and there were even rumors floating around that Bo would be starting the season down at Omaha, the Royals' Triple-A affiliate.

Bo had no intention of going back to the minors. He played brilliantly during spring training, and Gary Thurman went back to the bench.

Bo had a fine season in 1988. He was still striking out too much — 146 times over the year — but in every other category, he had improved a great deal. He became the first 25–25 player in Royals' history, hitting 25 homers, and stealing 27 bases. (José Canseco of the Oakland A's is famous for being the first 40–40 man in baseball history; if Bo continues to improve at the rate he has so far in his baseball career, he could become the first 50–50 man in baseball history.)

Bo's defensive skills had improved significantly, and he led the Royals with 11 outfield assists and made more than one circus catch along the way.

May was Bo's best month of the season, and he was chosen as Royals' Player of the Month. He hit

.330 in May, with 19 RBIs, five home runs, and nine stolen bases. But, on May 31, he tore his left hamstring in a game against the Cleveland Indians. It was a serious tear, and Bo didn't play again until July. Without that injury, Bo would probably have had an All-Star-caliber season.

He had several more single-game achievements during the 1988 season. He hit two home runs in a game against Seattle and had four-hit games against the Boston Red Sox on two separate occasions.

"He's a special athlete," Red Sox catcher Rich Gedman said later. "The thing that's most impressive is that he plays *two* professional sports. I think if he could concentrate on one or the other — in my eyes, it would be baseball, because there is less chance for injury — the type of athlete he is, he might be able to play for fifteen or twenty years. If he has a bad injury in football during the next two or three years, he might never find out what he could do in baseball."

In another game, against the Milwaukee Brewers, Bo stole three bases, gaining some more admirers. Increasingly, as Bo continued to achieve, Bo's fellow athletes were becoming just as awestruck as everyone else.

All-Star Milwaukee third baseman Paul Molitor is no exception to this. "Even though I've had the privilege of being a professional athlete for twelve years now," Molitor said in an interview some months later, "you still marvel at certain

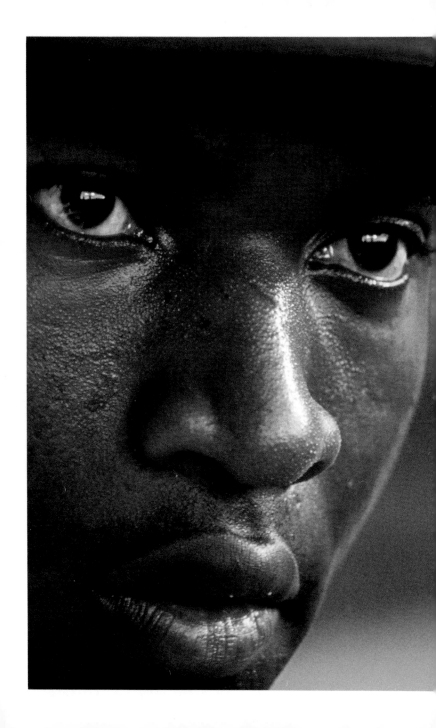

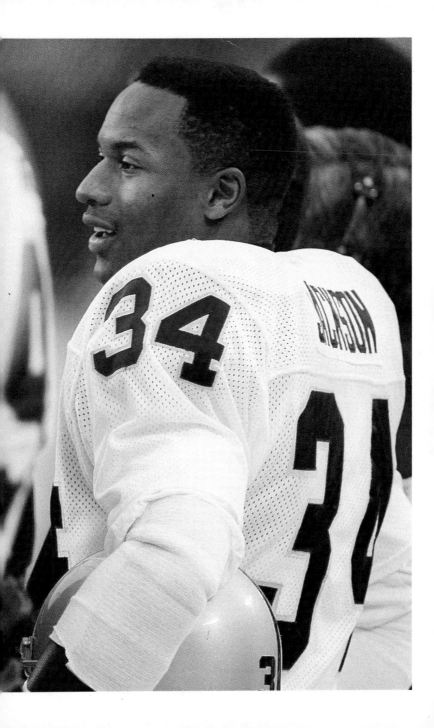

things. There's no question that Bo's an exception even to the best of professional athletes. What amazes me is all the things he has been able to achieve in such a short time. If he continues to improve in the way that he has, there's no telling what he might accomplish in this game. Not only is he gifted, but he's humble about what he does. He has the respect of his peers."

Cleveland third baseman Brook Jacoby put it even more simply. "He's just a phenomenal athlete," Brook said. "He's got speed, power; he's got baseball savvy. He's one-of-a-kind."

Every time Bo stepped onto an athletic field, it was getting harder and harder to find someone to disagree with that opinion.

9
On with the Show

After the baseball season, Bo took ten days off, and then reported to the Raiders. He looked over the new plays in the playbook, ran a few sprints, caught a few practice passes, and then said that he was ready to go. No one was going to argue with him.

Compared to his first season, Bo's 1988 football season was somewhat disappointing as he continued to be plagued by leg muscle pulls and tears. The most difficult part of playing two professional sports for Bo has been trying to stay healthy. If he ever gives up one of the two sports, that will be the most likely reason.

Bo's first game that year was against the Kansas City Chiefs. This year's game was much more successful than the one the year before when he had been injured on the very first play. This time, he gained 70 yards, and caught two passes for 10 more yards. The Raiders' new quarterback was Steve Beuerlein, who — so far — was playing quite well. Jay Schroeder, the Redskins' former star quarterback, had been expected to be the starter, but had been unable to deliver. Los Angeles beat Kansas City 27–7, and it seemed as though Bo had never left the football field.

The next game was against the New Orleans Saints, and Bo started off with a bang. He gained 25 yards sweeping around the right end, and then gained 20 more, going to the left. Unfortunately, on the next play, he felt a tightening in his left leg, and the Raiders decided not to take any chances with their young star. Bo spent the rest of the game on the bench. The Saints came away with the victory, by a score of 20–6. Without Bo, the Raiders just weren't the same team.

But Bo was ready to go the next Sunday against the Chiefs. Steve Beuerlein had a good day, throwing 18 passes for almost 250 yards, including one to Bo for 12 yards. Bo also gained 80 yards on the ground, including a 22-yard scamper for a touchdown. Teammate Marcus Allen chipped in with 70 of his own, and the Raiders won, 17–10.

They continued this happy trend the next week against the San Diego Chargers. Bo had a poor first half, gaining only 18 yards, and fumbling at a crucial moment. But he came back in the second half, catching two passes for 16 yards, and running for 46 more. On the day, he had 64 rushing yards, and the Raiders won, 13–3.

The next week they won again, defeating the mighty San Francisco 49ers, 6–3. This was the first time since 1977 that the 49ers had failed to score a touchdown in a game, and the Raider defense held them to only 83 yards on the ground. Bo gained 85 yards — more than all of the 49ers put together. On one play, he bulldozed right through ace San Francisco defensive back Ronnie Lott. When Bo ran someone over, the player knew that he had been hit.

The Raiders were on quite a high when they played the lowly Atlanta Falcons the following Sunday. But the Falcons burst their bubble swiftly. The entire Raider team played badly, and Bo had a career-low 25 yards rushing. (This does not, of course, include the game in his rookie season when he left with a sprained ankle early in the first quarter.) The Falcons won 12–6, and the Raiders' confidence was shaken.

Their next opponents, the Seattle Seahawks, took advantage of this, and Seattle quarterback Dave Krieg threw an impressive five touchdown passes. Raider quarterback Steve Beuerlein was only able to complete four passes all day, and Bo only gained 31 yards in 13 tries. The final 35–27 score sounds a lot closer than it really was.

It was December, and the Raiders played their

next game up in cold Buffalo. The Raiders' coaching staff decided to rest Beuerlein and give backup quarterback Jay Schroeder a chance, but in the icy weather, Jay fumbled twice. He was able to complete 14 passes, but the Raider defense gave up over 250 yards on the ground, and the Bills ran away with a 37–21 victory. Bo had an average — by his standards — day, gaining 64 yards in 12 attempts.

The team's final game that season was against the Seahawks, who picked up right where they had left off two weeks before. Dave Krieg threw four touchdown passes this time, and Seattle stormed their way to a 43–37 day. This was too bad, since it negated the fine day Jay Schroeder had, passing for three touchdowns of his own, and more than 350 total yards. Bo caught three of those passes for 14 yards, and ran for 67. It was a good effort, but the important thing was that his team had lost, and so, he couldn't be happy about his own performance.

During the entire season, Bo had only scored three touchdowns, and he vowed that he would do better in 1989. This answered the question the reporters were going to ask — Bo *was* going to continue his two-sport career.

Bo gained a total of 580 yards that season, with a 4.3-yard average. He had also caught nine passes, with an 8.7-yard average. Most athletes would have been satisfied with statistics like that.

Bo wasn't.

10
A Superstar Emerges

During the 1989 baseball season, Bo really showed what he could do. Almost every time he walked out onto the diamond, he did something amazing. He had become his own human highlight film.

Nineteen eighty-nine was a strange year for baseball, and Bo was one of the biggest — and nicest — stories. In a season that began with the Pete Rose controversy, followed by the death of baseball commissioner Bart Giamatti, and then ending with the earthquake during the World Series in San Francisco; Bo Jackson was a delightful story, indeed.

Bo's fame was growing beyond the boundaries of sports fans, and he had achieved one of the rarest levels of celebrity: instant recognition on a first-name basis. People know Madonna, and Cher, and Magic, and — Bo. One of the biggest factors contributing to this was Bo's highly successful series of print and television ads for Nike. "Bo knows" became a national catchphrase.

Crowds had now begun to gather — both at home and on the road — just to see Bo. Fans would come early to watch batting practice, and even players on the opposing teams would manage to find themselves out around the batting cage whenever Bo stepped inside. Everyone expected to see something new and amazing — and Bo was rarely one to disappoint.

He made his first big headline of the baseball season during spring training, hitting a home run reminiscent of the titanic shot he had hit back in college against the Georgia Bulldogs. The blow stunned even the most jaded of baseball observers.

It was a nice spring day in March, and the Royals were playing the Boston Red Sox at the Royals' Boardwalk and Baseball spring training complex and tourist attraction. Oil Can Boyd, Boston's joyfully eccentric pitcher, was on the mound that day. Bo's bat connected with Oil Can's slider, and the ball took off into the ozone layer, traveling an estimated 541 feet. The ball still seemed to be climbing when it cleared the 71-foot scoreboard.

Later that season, at Fenway Park, Oil Can was victimized by Bo again, as Bo smacked a home run to center field that hit the wall above the bleachers so hard that the whole park seemed to shake. Oil Can was probably relieved when he signed with Montreal over in the National League, and realized that he would no longer have to pitch to Bo Jackson.

"He's phenomenal," Boston catcher Rich Gedman said, shaking his head in admiration. "Every year that he's played in professional baseball, he's done nothing but get better. I just hope that we get the chance to see him for a long time because I think he's going to do some things no other athlete has ever done before."

Very few athletes ever hit a level where *other* athletes would be willing to pay to see them play. Bo was absolutely in that category. Players around the league often swapped Bo stories, each more incredible than the one before.

"He's such a great athlete," Royals' hitting coach Mike Lum said. "He has power better than anyone in the league, he runs faster than anyone, he has a better arm, and he's learning the game at this level. What I mean by that is, he's learning the pitchers. He's getting a pretty good idea of how they're trying to pitch him, and he's just going to get better."

Bo's happy manager, John Wathan, echoed his hitting coach's enthusiasm. "Most players have to go to the minor leagues and spend three or four years to be able to compete at the level of the big leagues," Wathan said, "and I think for Bo Jackson to do what he's done, at such a relatively young age, is a tremendous achievement. There's no telling how good he can be."

As the season went on, Bo continued writing his own legend. In May, he crunched a 461-foot home run off strikeout king Nolan Ryan. In Minnesota's "Homer-Dome," he sent a 402-foot homer up into the upper deck — the first time a right-handed batter had ever done such a thing in that stadium. Later, Bo was even overheard saying that he hadn't gotten good wood on the ball.

During batting practice, also in Minnesota, Bo sent a ball 450 feet into the stands. People were impressed. He hit the home run to the opposite field. People were even more impressed. He hit the home run *left*-handed. People were astounded.

Playing against the Orioles one night, Bo stepped out of the batter's box, trying to call time out. But the umpire didn't see him in time, and Baltimore pitcher Jeff Ballard threw the ball to the plate. Quickly Bo stepped back into the box, and without even getting both hands firmly on the bat, hit a home run into the left-field bleachers.

Playing the outfield, Bo continued to make acrobatic diving catches, and unbelievable throws. Perhaps the most unbelievable was in a game against Seattle. It was the tenth inning and the fleet-footed Harald Reynolds was on base. The next batter sent a shot out to the warning track in the deepest part of left field. Ordinarily, a turtle could score after a hit like that. Bo threw the ball 300 feet home — *without one bounce* — and right into catcher Bob Boone's glove. It is hard to say who was more surprised — Boone, when the ball slammed into his glove, or Reynolds, when he was tagged out at the plate. The fact that Reynolds would have scored the winning run made the play just that more dramatic.

Bo was still striking out more than he wanted to — he would have a major-league-leading 172 strikeouts during the season. But no one *reacted* to strikeouts quite the way Bo did.

After one strikeout, Bo was so upset that he broke his bat over his knee, shattering it like a tiny twig. King Kong might have had trouble doing such a thing, and Bo snapped the bat effortlessly.

That was pretty remarkable — if a little unnerving — but Bo went one better on another strikeout later in the season. *This* time, he was so frustrated with himself that he broke his bat over his own head. Anyone else who had attempted such a thing would probably have knocked him- or herself unconscious. Bo didn't even blink. Everyone else certainly did.

Then, in July, Bo was selected to the All-Star Game, where he was going to produce some happier memories for himself.

11
All-Star Hero

The 60th Annual All-Star Game was held on a warm California night in Anaheim. American League manager Tony LaRussa had already made headlines by announcing that Bo would be his leadoff batter. Normally a slugger like Bo would bat fourth or fifth, but LaRussa wanted to take advantage of Bo's blazing speed, and put him at the top of the lineup.

In the first inning, Bo walked up to the plate to face San Francisco's Rick Reuschel, who was having a superb season of his own. Bo swung, sending a pop fly into the air. The fly ball went higher and higher, and farther and farther, finally coming down in the middle of the green tarp beyond the center-field wall. This little pop fly traveled 448 feet — or one-and-a-half football fields. And Bo had, apparently, barely swung at it, just flicking the ball out there. Reuschel stood on the mound in something of a daze, then pitched to the next batter, Boston third baseman Wade Boggs, who also smacked a home run — a conventional home run.

Bo was only the ninth player in major league history to hit a home run in his first All-Star at bat. Other players to do this include Terry Steinbach of the Oakland A's in 1988, Lee Mazilli for the Mets in 1979, and Johnny Bench for the Reds in 1969. It was also the first home run hit to lead off an All-Star Game since Joe Morgan, the Cincinnati Reds' Hall of Famer, led off the All-Star Game with a roundtripper back in 1977.

Bo was only getting started. The next time he came up, he hit a grounder to the infield, allowing a runner on third to score. When the Cubs' Ryne Sandberg was unable to complete the double play, Bo ended up at first. He promptly stole second base. Now, in and of itself, that is not all that remarkable. However, Bo became only the second baseball player in history to hit a home run and steal a base in the same All-Star Game. The other player who did that was Willie Mays, back in 1962. Bo was in pretty good company.

The American League won the game, by a score of 5–3, and Bo was selected as the Most Valuable Player. He had also had a single in the game, off Expos ace Tim Burke.

Bo's second half of the season was not quite as good as his first half, mainly because he continued to have various muscle pulls and strains in his legs. In each of his baseball seasons thus far, his first half has been significantly better than his second half, and some people feel that this is because Bo just gets worn out by the end of the year. Either way, Bo completed the season with a nifty collection of statistics. His final batting average was .256, an improvement over the year before.

For the second season in a row, Bo was a 25–25 man, with 32 home runs in 1989, and 26 stolen bases. Thirty-two home runs was the fourth highest total in the American League, and his 105 RBIs was also the fourth highest in the league. Bo averaged one home run for every 16 times at bat, which was the third highest ratio in the league. He got an RBI every 4.9 at bats, which led the entire American League.

Bo also led the Royals in several categories. He had the highest slugging percentage at .495. (This figure is determined by dividing the number of times at bat into the number of total bases a player reaches. Power hitters have much higher slugging percentages than singles hitters.) Bo also scored the most runs — 86, and had the most total bases with 255.

Although Bo led the majors in strikeouts, he was encouraged to find that his *rate* of striking out had decreased from once every two-and-a-half at bats to once every 3.4 plate appearances.

Another interesting statistic emerged. Baseball is a game where everyone involved is always coming up with new statistics. This particular statistic was the run production average, which was determined by adding the number of runs scored and the number of runs batted in, and then dividing that by the number of plate appearances. Kevin Mitchell of the San Francisco Giants led the majors with a .352 run production average, and Bo came in second with a .340 average. Bo's average the previous season had been .280, which made him twenty-third in the majors.

It also turned out that Bo was the best hitter in the American League on the road, leading the league with 59 road RBIs, and tying Mark McGwire of the A's with 21 road game home runs.

After the season, Bo placed tenth in the voting for the American League's Most Valuable Player Award. Many people felt that he should have placed even higher.

Bo was eligible for arbitration after the 1989 season, and he decided that he wanted a raise large enough to put him in the same category as other star third-year players. He and his agent requested a raise to $1,900,001, which is not as high as it seems in a sport where a number of players are making more than three million dollars a year. In fan attendance alone, Bo is worth a fortune.

However, the Royals only offered him (only!) a million dollars, and the salary arbitrator found in favor of the team. Certainly, in years to come, Bo's salary will rise to the level of other superstars like Don Mattingly, Rickey Henderson, and Kirby Puckett.

Bo's peers in the American League continued to be amazed, and excited, by Bo's success.

"He's a great talent, I'll tell you that," New York Yankees first baseman Don Mattingly said in an interview. "A guy who runs like that, throws well, great power — he's just got great potential. This is the first year that he's really had a full season without getting hurt, and he had a great year. He'd be an even greater player if he spent all of his time playing baseball."

Dave Henderson, the clutch-hitting center fielder for the Oakland A's, was in complete agreement. "Well," he said, in a dugout interview late in the season, "Bo was a real raw talent — in baseball, that is — and he taught himself the game, and now he's one of the great players in pro ball. He's one of the guys we all admire. Because all of us played football and baseball, but somewhere along the line, we had to give it up because we couldn't do both. But, he's done both on a professional level and — it's almost inconceivable."

Frank White, the Royals' second baseman, just laughed when he was asked what he thought about Bo. "Everything there is to say has already been said," he said. "I don't have a big enough vocabulary."

No one has a big enough vocabulary to describe Bo Jackson.

12
Bo Still Knows Football

After the baseball season ended, Bo took his usual ten days off before he went to join the Raiders. When asked when Bo was going to report, the Raiders' ownership admitted that they hadn't heard from him. They also admitted that neither they, nor the Royals' owners, had Bo's home telephone number. If they wanted to talk to him, they had to call his agent, Richard Woods, down in Alabama. As usual, when it came to Bo, rules were made to be broken.

Before Bo arrived to join the football team, the Raiders had won two games, and lost three. Coach Flores had been fired, and replaced by former Raiders star Art Shell. Coach Shell was the first black head coach ever to be hired in the NFL, as sports management positions continue to be slow to catch up to the rest of society.

Bo's first game back was against those old friends, the Kansas City Chiefs. The Raiders won, 20–14. Bo gained 85 yards, including a 45-yard sprint past Chiefs All-Pro defensive back Deron Cherry. He also bulled forward for an old-fashioned rock-'em-sock-'em two-yard touchdown run. Once again, Bo had returned to football as though he had never left.

It was Coach Shell's second game at the helm — and his second victory. He was very pleased to have a running back who could wander cheerfully into the locker room on a Wednesday after months away from the game and score a touchdown four days later. Bo is a walking example of why training camp may be less important than people think. Professional sports have advanced to a level where most athletes can probably accomplish more by training on their own time, at their own pace. At any rate, Bo Jackson certainly can. (What exactly is it that he does on those ten days off — eat kryptonite?)

Next, the Raiders played the Philadelphia Eagles, suffering a tough 10–7 defeat. Kicker Jeff Jaeger missed two easy field goals, which was the difference in the game for the Raiders. Bo carried the ball 20 times, grinding out 79 yards. His longest run of the day was 18 yards.

The following Sunday, the Raiders faced the Washington Redskins, steamrolling to a 37–24 victory. Steve Beuerlein, quarterbacking for Los Angeles again, had a good day, passing for two touchdowns. Bo also scored a touchdown, on a brilliant 73-yard run, outdistancing the entire Redskin defense. Bo had a total of 144 yards that day, and the home crowd at the LA Coliseum went home happy. Bo had also run for a 45-yard touchdown, but the officials called it back because of a holding penalty against one of Bo's teammates.

The Raiders, with their new coach and their late-arriving running back, were on a roll. They crushed the Cincinnati Bengals by a score of 28–7 the next week. Bo had another one of those "you had to see it to believe it" games, very much like his performance against the Seahawks during his rookie season.

This time, barely three minutes into the game, Bo had already leapt over the Bengals' defensive line, landing in the end zone with a seven-yard-touchdown score. A few minutes later, Bo outdid even himself. He scored a 92-yard touchdown, breaking his own Raiders' record run of 91 yards. By doing so, Bo became the first player in the history of professional football to make *two* 90-plus-yard runs in his career. O.J. Simpson hadn't done it; Walter Payton hadn't done it; Jim Brown hadn't done it. Once again, Bo had vaulted into a class all by himself. And he had done this only 20 games into his professional career. Not only did Bo know football, but he had possibly *reinvented* football.

Bo finished the afternoon with 159 total yards, with a 12.2 yards-per-carry average. The Raiders finished with another victory.

The next week, the Raiders faced the San Diego Chargers, and came away with a disappointing loss. Late in the third quarter, the team had been leading the Chargers by a 12–0 margin, but the Chargers came back to win the game on a 91-yard kickoff return for a touchdown, and then another touchdown halfway through the fourth quarter.

Even so, Bo rushed for another 103 yards, and also caught two passes for 18 yards. The difference in the game came when quarterback Jay Schroeder threw three interceptions.

A week later, Los Angeles was soundly defeated by the Houston Oilers. Houston quarterback Warren Moon was terrific, completing 20 passes for almost 250 yards, including a 25-yard touchdown pass. Bo was only able to gain 54 yards all day, most of which came in the first half. He also caught two passes for five yards, but it wasn't a day to remember. Los Angeles quarterback Steve Beuerlein threw three interceptions — as Schroeder had the week before. The Raiders also fumbled twice, the Oilers recovering both times.

The team's next game was against Denver, and they had to win to keep their play-off hopes alive.

Bo had another strong game, and kicker Jeff Jaeger booted the winning field goal in overtime, giving the Raiders a 16–13 victory. The Broncos had had a chance to win in the last minute of the fourth quarter, but John Elway threw an interception to Raider defenseman Lionel Washington, and the game went to overtime.

Next came the Phoenix Cardinals, and once again, the Raiders had to win to stay in the play-off race. Marcus Allen was the big hero of the day, making a one-yard dive for the winning touchdown with less than a minute remaining in the game. The final score was 16–14. So far, Allen had only gained nine yards all day — but that tenth yard was the most crucial one of the game.

Bo rushed for a solid 114 yards, a feat he was now making seem routine. Marcus Allen was now being used almost exclusively as a blocking back.

The Raiders' final two games of the season were against the Seattle Seahawks and the New York Giants. They tried as hard as they could, but lost both games, ruining their chances to go to the play-offs. The loss to Seattle was particularly critical, since the Raiders and the Seahawks are both in the same division. The team finished with an 8–8 record, and would have to wait until the 1990 season to try again.

Bo finished the year with a total of 570 yards. He now had a career average of 5.6 yards per carry — the highest such average in NFL history.

Bo had hoped very much to be selected to play in the Pro Bowl, but he was passed over, and that, too, would have to wait for another season.

When the next season came around, Bo would be ready.

13
How Far Can Bo Go?

There seems to be little doubt that Bo can pretty much write his own ticket. Certainly, if he ever decides to concentrate on just one sport, he will break most of the records in the book. If he *doesn't* decide to concentrate on one sport, he will just break *some* of the records. Either way, it is a safe bet that Bo will continue to tantalize and excite sports fans for many years to come.

The only question anyone has about Bo anymore concerns his durability. In each of his seasons, he has had some sort of injury. Critics note that former running backs Walter Payton and Jim Brown missed a combined total of one game in their careers. Bo has also spent time on the disabled list while playing baseball.

It is possible that Bo gets injured because not

even the strongest human body can take the stresses of two professional sports, but it is also possible that Bo is just plain smart enough to admit when he's hurt, instead of trying to play through injuries and making them worse. Regardless, Bo probably knows what he is doing, and people should just let him do it.

One thing Bo is doing is going back to school to complete his studies. Athletes who leave college early often say that they will return one day, but they rarely do. As a rule, the more successful an athlete becomes, the less likely he or she is to finish school. Bo, typically, is the exception to this. He has always said that he wants to work with children when he retires from sports — and Bo generally does what he says he's going to do.

"It doesn't happen too often that a guy can come along, and be able to do what Bo has done," Kansas City manager John Wathan remarked in a mid-baseball-season interview. "He's got all the tools, so there's no telling what Bo Jackson will have accomplished when he decides to give up the game of baseball. Obviously, selfishly, we'd like him to quit football and just play baseball, but I don't know if that's going to happen. He's been able to do them both so far, and we've been able to live with it."

Royals' bullpen closer Jeff Montgomery was able to put it even more simply. "It's a honor to play with a guy like Bo Jackson," he said. "It's a lot of fun to come out and see him do his heroics, day after day. He's done a lot of things people never really thought *could* be done. It's fun to watch, and it's exciting."

Bo Jackson *is* exciting. Bo Jackson is an original. Athletes and fans alike can only hope that Bo stays around for a very long time. He is one in a million.

Bo Jackson's
Awards and Honors

High School

Selected as an All-State Athlete, Alabama, in football, baseball, and track

Alabama high school decathlon champion his junior and senior years

Holder of state records in the 60- and 120-yard hurdles, the 60- and 100-yard dashes, the long jump, the high jump, and the decathlon

National high school home run record, 20 home runs in one season, senior year

College

Lettered in football, baseball, indoor and outdoor track

Two-time semifinalist, NCAA track championships

Most Valuable Player, Sugar Bowl, 1983

Three-time All-America in football

Most Valuable Player, Liberty Bowl, 1984

Walter Camp Trophy for most outstanding college football player in the country, 1985

Heisman Trophy for the best college player in the country, 1985

Professional Football

First pick in the 1986 football draft, Tampa Bay Buccaneers

Selected by the Los Angeles Raiders, 1987 NFL draft

Unanimous selection, NFL All-Rookie Team, 1987

Only player in the history of the NFL to have two touchdown runs longer than 90 yards

Professional Baseball

Selected by the Kansas City Royals, fourth round, 1986 baseball free-agent draft

First player in Royals' history to go from the college campus to the big league club in one year

Southern League (AA) Player of the Week, July 15–21, 1986

Royals' Player of the Month, May 1988

Most Valuable Player, 1989 Baseball All-Star Game

Ninth player in baseball history to hit a home run in his first All-Star at bat

Second player in baseball history to hit a home run and steal a base in the same All-Star Game

Bo Jackson's Career Statistics Through 1989 Season

College Football

Games	Total Yards	Yards per Game	Avg. Carry	TDs
38	4,303	113.2	6.6	45

College Baseball

Games	Batting Average	Home Runs	RBI
89	.335	28	70

Professional Football

Year	Carries	Total Yards	Avg. Yards per Carry	TDs
1987	81	554	6.8	4
1988	136	580	4.3	3
1989	84	570	6.8	4
Totals	301	1,704	5.9	11

Professional Baseball

Year-Club	Avg.	G	AB	R	H	HR	RBI	SO	SB
1986									
Memphis	.277	53	184	30	51	7	25	81	3
Kansas City	.207	25	82	9	17	2	9	34	3
1987									
Kansas City	.235	116	396	46	93	22	53	158	10
1988									
Kansas City	.246	124	439	63	108	25	68	146	27
1989									
Kansas City	.256	135	515	86	132	32	105	172	26
Major League Totals	.244	400	1432	204	350	81	235	510	66